THE ELEMENTS

Aluminum

John Farndon

BENCHMARK BOOKS

MARSHALL CAVENDISH
NEW YORK

Benchmark Books
Marshall Cavendish Corporation
99 White Plains Road
Tarrytown, New York 10591

Library of Congress Cataloging-in-Publication Data
Farndon, John.
Aluminum / John Farndon.
p.   cm. — (The elements)
Includes index.
Summary: Describes the discovery, versatility and other special characteristics,
various uses, and affect on the human body of this most common metal in the world.
ISBN 0-7614-0947-5 (lib. bdg.)
1. Aluminum—Juvenile literature. [1. Aluminum.] I. Title.
II. Elements (Benchmark Books)
QD181.A4 F37 2001
546'.673—dc21   99-049671 CIP AC

Printed in Hong Kong

Picture credits
Front cover: Gary Gladstone/Image Bank.
Back cover: James L. Amos/Corbis (UK) Ltd.
Corbis (UK) Ltd.: Archivo Iconografico 5; Bettmann 11; Howard Davies 8; José Manuel Sanchis Calvete *iii*, 18;
James L. Amos 10, 30; Paul A. Souders *i*, 4, 22; Roger Ressmeyer 14; Stephanie Maze 27 (*right*).
Image Bank: Arthur Meyerson 24; David Vance 26; Gary Gladstone 12; T. Anderson 21.
Image Select: Ann Ronan 9.
Leslie Garland Picture Library: Brian Gadsby 13.
Science Photo Library: Alex Bartel 25; Alfred Pasieka 27 (*left*); Ben Johnson 7; Chris Knapton 19;
Crown Copyright/Health & Safety Laboratory 16; Manfred Kage 15; Royal Observatory, Edinburgh/AAO 6.
Travel Ink: David Toase 20.

Series created by Brown Partworks Ltd.
Designed by wda

Contents

What is aluminum?

Stacks of shiny aluminum alloy bars at a metal refinery in Kitimat, British Columbia.

Aluminum is the most common metal in the world and, after silicon and oxygen, is the third most abundant element of all. Around 8 percent of Earth's outer layer (crust) is made up of aluminum. Despite its abundance, humans only discovered aluminum in the 19th century. Unlike metals such as gold and silver, aluminum never occurs alone in nature. Instead, it forms compounds with other elements. To reveal the pure metal, these compounds must be broken down by an industrial process called refining, which requires a huge amount of energy.

Aluminum is a shiny, silvery metal. It is extremely light and so soft that a thick sheet can be bent easily by hand. When exposed to the air, the surface of the metal reacts with oxygen to form an aluminum oxide coating, preventing further corrosion of the metal underneath.

All these properties make aluminum a very important element. Its uses range from making chewing gum wrappers and beverage cans to armor-plating for tanks and airplane bodies. Indeed, the modern world would be a very different place without aluminum.

The aluminum atom

Every atom contains even smaller particles called protons, neutrons, and electrons. The protons and neutrons cluster together in the nucleus at the center of an atom. The electrons spin around the nucleus in a series of layers called electron shells.

The number of protons is given by the atomic number. Aluminum has an atomic number of 13, so there are 13 protons in each atom. The protons and neutrons combine to give the atom its mass. Aluminum has an atomic mass of 27, which means each atom has 14 neutrons. The numbers of electrons and protons are always equal, so there are 13 electrons in each atom of aluminum.

A 15th-century manuscript depicts a laborer extracting alum from the ground using a pickax.

ALUMINUM ATOM

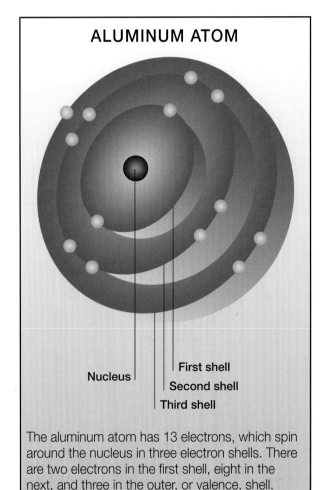

Nucleus

First shell

Second shell

Third shell

The aluminum atom has 13 electrons, which spin around the nucleus in three electron shells. There are two electrons in the first shell, eight in the next, and three in the outer, or valence, shell.

DID YOU KNOW?

ROMAN POWDER

The word *aluminum* comes from the Latin *alumen,* meaning "alum." Alum is a white powder containing aluminum and often other metals such as potassium. Ancient Roman surgeons applied alum to wounds soldiers suffered in battle. It acted as an astringent, drying the wounds and drawing the tissue together so the wound could heal. Alum was also used by the Babylonians to make dyes stick to fabrics. In the Middle Ages, alum was used to cure (dry) the skins of dead animals. Today, the most common use is in the papermaking industry.

Where aluminum is found

Small quantities of aluminum are found throughout the universe. In fact, around 2,000 atoms in every billion in the universe are aluminum. Most of the aluminum found on Earth probably formed at least five billion years ago in the heart of a red giant star. Inside this star, the nuclei of many helium atoms were fused together by the enormous pressures and temperatures to make heavier elements such as aluminum.

The world we live in formed from the remains of such a giant star. As the hot young Earth slowly cooled, heavy

An optical image of the red giant star Antares. Many scientists believe that the aluminum found on our own planet formed during the collapse of a similar star some five billion years ago.

DID YOU KNOW?

CORUNDUM

Sometimes, boiling-hot, mineral-rich water seeps through the cracks in cooling igneous rocks. This water often contains aluminum oxide, which, as it crystallizes, forms one of the hardest minerals of all—corundum. Only diamond is harder than corundum, which makes corundum perfect for use as an abrasive powder (emery) for sharpening knives and sanding tools. However, corundum is not just useful as an abrasive. In the right circumstances it can crystallize into some of the world's most beautiful and precious gems—red rubies and blue sapphires. Ruby is mainly aluminum oxide with tiny traces of chromium. Sapphire is aluminum oxide with traces of iron and titanium.

Aluminum in the ground

Since it is the most common metal in the world, it follows that most minerals, rocks, and soils are rich in compounds containing aluminum. Igneous rocks develop from molten rock, either volcanic lava on Earth's surface or magma deep underground. Granites and dolerites are examples of igneous rocks. These rocks are rich in minerals such as feldspars and

elements, such as iron, sank to the core. Aluminum was so light it floated up to the surface to form the solid crust, along with the elements silicon and oxygen.

A sample of bauxite, the raw material from which the metal aluminum is extracted. Its red color is due to the presence of iron oxide impurities.

micas, which are made mainly from aluminum and silicon compounds. Over time, heavy rains break these rocks down into powder, forming clays equally rich in minerals containing aluminum hydroxide ($Al[OH]_3$), such as boehmite, diaspore, and gibbsite. In warm, moist climates, the clays gradually break down to form thick sheets of bauxite, the raw material from which aluminum is extracted. Bauxite deposits are the major source of aluminum ores.

Bauxite

Bauxite is mostly aluminum hydroxide, made from about two-thirds alumina (aluminum oxide; Al_2O_3) and about a

Aluminum-rich bauxite ore is loaded onto a dumpster truck in a mine in Jamaica.

quarter water. Alumina is the compound from which aluminum is refined. Bauxite also contains other compounds, such as titanium oxide (TiO_2) and silica (SiO_2).

The largest bauxite deposits are found in Australia, Brazil, Guinea, Jamaica, and Surinam. Bauxite deposits are fairly easy to extract because they are found near the surface of the soil. Bulldozers move in to clear away the vegetation and topsoil, and the bauxite is broken up with explosives. Finally, powerful mechanical diggers shovel the bauxite into trucks and trains.

The discovery of aluminum

People have been using alum powder for more than 5,000 years. However, it was only when Prussian chemist Johann Pott prepared the compound alumina (aluminum oxide) from alum powder in the mid-18th century that scientists began to realize that alumina was a compound of oxygen and an unknown and important metallic element. Early in the 19th century, British chemist Sir Humphry Davy (1778–1829) began to examine this unknown quantity of alumina and dubbed the mystery metal "aluminum." The name has stuck in the United States, but in Europe the name was changed slightly to "aluminium" soon after Davy's death.

In 1809, Davy made the first real breakthrough in the hunt for aluminum. Davy managed to make an alloy (mixture) of aluminum with iron by using electrical energy to heat alumina, iron, and carbon. Sixteen years later, Danish

A series of furnaces is used to prepare aluminum using the Hall-Héroult process. Hall and Héroult discovered the process independently in 1886.

physicist Hans Christian Oersted (1777–1851) managed to prepare the first ever sample of pure aluminum. First, he used alumina to make aluminum chloride ($AlCl_3$). Then he heated the aluminum chloride with an alloy of potassium and

The aluminum and gold baby rattle ordered by French emperor Napoléon III for his son Prince Louis Napoleon in 1856.

mercury. As more heat was applied to the mixture, Oersted noticed that a small lump of aluminum began to form in the alloy. Although it was a fairly impure and powdery sample, it was definitely the elusive new metal aluminum.

Just two years later, German chemist Friedrich Wöhler (1800–1882) prepared minute grains of pure aluminum by heating aluminum chloride to melting point with potassium. Wöhler continued his experiments for almost 20 years. They finally paid off when, in 1845, he managed to isolate globules of pure aluminum. They were no bigger than pinheads, but they were big enough to be weighed and studied. What Wöhler found about the metal was a revelation. Aluminum was one of the lightest of all metals. It was soft, easy to shape, and never seemed to corrode.

In 1854, French scientist Henri Étienne Sainte-Claire Deville (1818–1881) realized he could extract more aluminum from aluminum chloride by using sodium in place of potassium. At first, Deville made marble-sized balls of pure aluminum, but he improved his method, resulting in the preparation of huge bars of the metal. Deville exhibited his

U.S. chemist Charles Martin Hall (pictured above), along with French metallurgist Paul-Louis-Toussaint Héroult, is credited with inventing the process for making aluminum.

aluminum, as well as dinner spoons and a baby's rattle. Deville improved his technique, and the price of aluminum went down from $115 per pound to $17 per pound by 1859. However, it was still too expensive for everyday use.

The aluminum industry begins

Two dramatic breakthroughs in the 1880s heralded the start of the aluminum industry. In 1886, U.S. chemist Charles Martin Hall (1863–1914) and French metallurgist Paul-Louis-Toussaint Héroult (1863–1914) found a way of making aluminum in bulk by using electricity. The second breakthrough was the discovery of a cheap way of extracting alumina from bauxite in 1888 by German chemist Karl Joseph Bayer. Both Bayer's method and Hall and Héroult's (now known as the Hall-Héroult process) are explained in detail from pages 21 through 23.

aluminum bars at the 1855 Paris Exposition, and thousands of people queued up to get a glimpse of the new metal. At this time, aluminum was more valuable than silver because it was so expensive to produce. Aluminum became reserved only for those who could afford it. French emperor Napoléon III (1808–1873) commissioned a breastplate made of

DID YOU KNOW?

THE HYDROELECTRIC AGE
The industrial preparation of aluminum depends on hydroelectricity—electricity generated by falling water. The very first hydroelectric plant was a tiny private plant built in Northumberland, England, in 1880. In 1887, the first commercial hydroelectric plant started to produce aluminum at the famous waterfalls of Neuheusen on the Rhine River, Germany.

Special characteristics

Aluminum beverage containers have replaced the more traditional tin-plated steel cans.

Aluminum is an extremely versatile metal, which is why it has many different uses. It is one of the lightest of all metals, weighing just 170 lbs. per cubic ft (2,700 kg/m^3)—about one third as heavy as steel. Aluminum can be made even lighter by mixing it with the metal lithium. This saves so much weight that the mixture is used not only for building airplanes, automobiles, and buses, but anything where strength is not absolutely vital but a reduction in weight is a real bonus. Makers of soft drinks, for example, make use of the metal's lightness in beverage containers. Aluminum containers are cheap to ship because they are so light.

Aluminum is also extremely resistant to corrosion. As soon as it is exposed to air, the surface of the metal quickly tarnishes with a coat of white aluminum oxide (Al_2O_3), protecting the metal from further attack by pollution, rain, and the wind. This is another reason why aluminum is perfect for airplane parts, automobile bodies, and other structures designed to be exposed to the elements.

One major drawback of aluminum is its softness. While this makes it easy to shape, it can be a disadvantage where overall strength is needed. However, aluminum can be made almost as strong as steel by alloying it with other metals. Airplane parts are often made of such alloys.

ALUMINUM FACTS

⊙ Aluminum reflects 80 percent of the light that hits it. This is why it is often used as a reflector in light fittings.

⊙ Since aluminum reflects heat so well, it is used to make firefighters' flameproof suits.

⊙ In small quantities aluminum is nontoxic. As a result, it is used for food and drink containers.

⊙ Aluminum melts at 1,220°F (660°C) and boils at 4,472°F (2,467°C).

⊙ The relative density of aluminum is 2.7; that is, it is 2.7 times as dense as water. Its absolute density is 170 lbs. per cubic ft (2,700 kg/m^3).

⊙ Aluminum is 2.75 on the Mohs' (hardness) scale, between gypsum and calcite.

Aluminum is one of the best conductors of electricity and heat. Indeed, it is such a good conductor of heat that it is often used to make saucepans, not only because it is cheap but because it transmits heat efficiently and cools down quickly.

Aluminum is one of only three metals, along with copper and silver, to be used to make electrical conduction wires. Aluminum is just under two-thirds as good a conductor as copper, but it is so light that it more than makes up for this in applications where weight is important. For example, aluminum is widely used for overhead power cables.

These overhead power cables are made of a steel cable core surrounded by twisted strands of aluminum metal.

A highly reactive element

Aluminum is a very reactive metal. Atoms with incompletely filled electron shells will generally either give up those electrons to other atoms, forming ions, or join with other atoms in what are called covalent bonds to completely fill the outer shell with shared electrons. Since aluminum has only three electrons in an outer shell that can potentially hold eight, it reacts readily with other atoms. This is why aluminum is almost always found in compounds, such as alumina (Al_2O_3).

A layer of aluminum oxide forms when aluminum is exposed to the air. Substances that eat through this layer, such as dilute acids and strong alkalis, can react with the metal underneath. For example, hydrochloric acid (HCl), will dissolve the metal, making salts and hydrogen. As a result, acidic fruit juices are never stored in aluminum containers. Sodium hydroxide (NaOH), a strong alkali, also reacts with aluminum, making sodium aluminate ($NaAl[OH]_4$) and hydrogen (H_2). This is why alkaline detergents should not be used to clean aluminum saucepans.

Surprisingly, when heated, oxidizing acids, such as nitric acid (HNO_3), only

A giant mirror from Hale Telescope in San Diego is cleaned before applying a new coat of aluminum to its surface. A sample of highly refined aluminum is vaporized and then deposited onto the mirror, coating the entire surface of the glass. Aluminum's reflective properties make it ideal for this application.

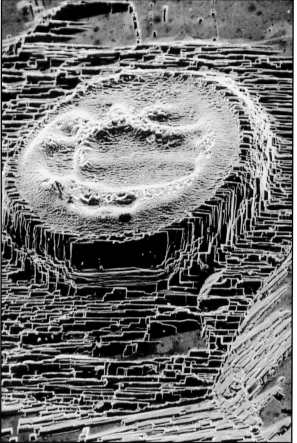

A scanning electron micrograph reveals the surface detail of a sample of high-purity aluminum.

react a little with aluminum. This is because an oxide layer rapidly coats the surface of the metal and stops the reaction. For this reason, nitric acid can actually be shipped in tanks made from aluminum. If, on the other hand, aluminum is heated—especially in powdered form—the metal reacts strongly with carbon, chlorine, nitrogen, phosphorus, and sulfur. Aluminum powder burns in carbon monoxide (CO) or carbon dioxide (CO_2) to form alumina and carbide (Al_4C_3).

ATOMS AT WORK

One molecule of hydrochloric acid consists of an atom of hydrogen attached to an atom of chlorine. If hydrochloric acid is heated slightly, it can break through aluminum's protective coat of aluminum oxide, provoking a strong reaction. Indeed, aluminum dissolves rapidly in hydrochloric acid and hydrogen gas is given off.

Hydrogen | Chlorine

Hydrochloric acid
HCl

Six hydrochloric acid molecules react with two aluminum atoms.

6x HCl

2x Al

Three chlorine atoms bond with an aluminum atom to form one aluminum chloride molecule. Hydrogen atoms bond to form hydrogen gas.

Hydrogen gas
3x H_2

Aluminum chloride
2x $AlCl_3$

The chemical reaction that takes place can be written like this:

$$2Al + 6HCl \rightarrow 2AlCl_3 + 3H_2$$

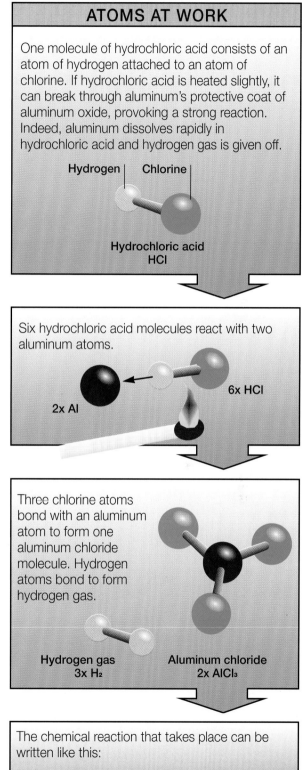

Ionic or covalent?

The three electrons in the outer electron shell of an aluminum atom should make the metal a "trivalent ion," which means that the atom should lose these "spare" electrons and make an ionic bond with certain other elements.

However, many aluminum compounds are covalent. Here, the aluminum ion shares only a single electron with other ions. For example, when aluminum combines with hydrogen, one aluminum ion joins with

Sparks form as an aluminum wrench strikes a block of rusty iron (iron oxide). This reaction—the Thermit process—generates an enormous amount of heat.

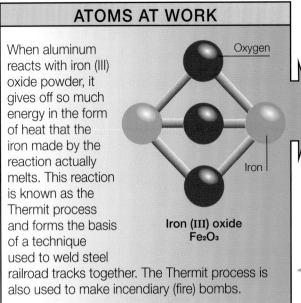

ATOMS AT WORK

When aluminum reacts with iron (III) oxide powder, it gives off so much energy in the form of heat that the iron made by the reaction actually melts. This reaction is known as the Thermit process and forms the basis of a technique used to weld steel railroad tracks together. The Thermit process is also used to make incendiary (fire) bombs.

Oxygen

Iron

Iron (III) oxide
Fe₂O₃

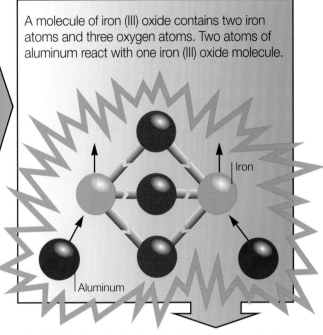

A molecule of iron (III) oxide contains two iron atoms and three oxygen atoms. Two atoms of aluminum react with one iron (III) oxide molecule.

Iron

Aluminum

three hydrogen ions, forming the covalent molecule AlH_3. This means even with the shared electrons Al^{3+} gets from hydrogen, the ion still only has six electrons in its outer shell. This is two short of the full complement of eight, so these molecules typically join together to make polymers.

When an aluminum atom becomes an Al^{3+} ion, it loses a tiny negative charge and becomes a positively charged ion. When it comes into contact with other, negative, ions, Al^{3+} tends to draw electrons toward it, making the combination of ions more positive at one end and more negative at the other. This effect is called polarization. Water (H_2O) is a polar molecule, but when it meets an aluminum ion, the polarizing effect of the Al^{3+} ion weakens the bonds in the water molecule and draws the oxygen atoms toward it.

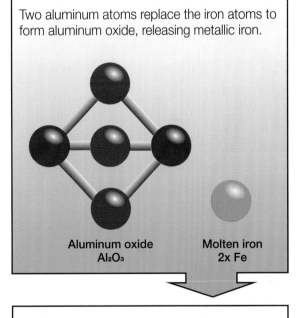

Two aluminum atoms replace the iron atoms to form aluminum oxide, releasing metallic iron.

Aluminum oxide
Al₂O₃

Molten iron
2x Fe

The chemical reaction that takes place in the Thermit process can be written like this:

$$2Al + Fe_2O_3 \rightarrow Al_2O_3 + 2Fe$$

The number of atoms on each side of the equation is the same, although the atoms have joined up in new combinations.

Aluminum compounds

Aluminum oxide (Al_2O_3) is a white compound that forms a visible layer on the surface of aluminum when it is exposed to air. In its hydrated (water-

A sample of amethyst taken from a mine in Guerrero, Mexico. Amethyst is made of a mineral called corundum. Its vivid coloration is a result of impurities such as iron oxide.

containing) form it is also known as alumina ($Al_2O_3.3H_2O$), another white substance used in huge quantities for all kinds of different tasks.

Naturally, alumina is found in a number of different forms, both as crystals and as powders. When alumina crystallizes, for example, it forms corundum, a mineral that is the basis of the gemstones amethyst, ruby, and sapphire. As powders, the different forms of alumina are very tough and unreactive. They are used where a substance is needed to contain or insulate a particular process. Alumina is extremely common and is found in the soil as the ore bauxite. Alumina can also be made in a laboratory by heating aluminum hydroxide to drive off the water. The difference between the forms often hinges on the way the water content has been driven off.

In "activated" alumina, the water is driven off at a fairly low temperature. Activated alumina has an amazing ability to reabsorb water, and it is used widely as a drying agent in oil refining and the petrochemical industry.

In "calcined" alumina, the oxide has been heated to over 1,920°F (1,050°C) to drive off the water. The result is a very pure form of aluminum oxide powder, which is almost as hard as corundum. It is also very resistant to

Alumina is used to make electrical insulators. These are designed to prevent the discharge of electricity to the ground or nearby objects.

electricity. This is why it is used to make the insulators in car spark plugs and high-voltage electricity supplies. It is also used to make aluminum.

The oxide known as "tabular" alumina is heated to over 3,000°F (1,650°C) to make very tough, heat-resistant crystals. These crystals are shaped into bricks and used to line furnaces and kilns for making glass and porcelain.

Aluminum hydroxide

Aluminum hydroxide (Al[OH]$_3$) is a white, jellylike substance formed when a small amount of alkali is added to an aluminum salt. The removal of a molecule of water results in the mineral boehmite (AlO[OH]), which occurs naturally in the aluminum ore bauxite. The original Al(OH)$_3$ structure is kept in gibbsite, another mineral found in bauxite. In industry, gibbsite is a very important mineral, forming the basis of most toothpastes as well as the antacid tablets used to counteract indigestion. Gibbsite is also widely used in the china, glass, papermaking, petroleum, and rubber industries.

Aluminum chloride

Aluminum chloride (AlCl$_3$) occurs as a white solid. The compound is prepared in a laboratory by passing dry chlorine gas or dry hydrogen chloride gas over a heated sample of metallic aluminum.

An important reaction of aluminum chloride is its hydrolysis by water. As a result, the compound turns to fumes when in contact with moist air and is a major ingredient in many deodorants.

Toothpaste often contains small quantities of aluminum hydroxide (Al[OH]$_3$), or gibbsite. Gibbsite helps counteract the buildup of acids that destroy the enamel layer that covers our teeth.

How aluminum is made

Each year, around 23 million tons (21 million tonnes) of aluminum is made all over the world. The United States and Canada dominate the aluminum industry; 20 percent of the world's aluminum supply comes from the United States alone. Two processes are used to extract aluminum from its ore, bauxite.

The Bayer process

The Bayer process is used to refine bauxite into almost pure alumina (hydrated aluminum oxide; Al_2O_3). First, bauxite is mixed with sodium hydroxide (NaOH) and water (H_2O) at high pressure and temperature. This results in a boiling hot solution of sodium aluminate ($NaAl[OH]_4$), which is then drained into settling tanks. Here, impurities are filtered from the mix. The resulting liquid is pumped into cooling vats. As the solution cools, aluminum hydroxide ($Al[OH]_3$) crystals form. These are washed and heat-dried in kilns (ovens) at temperatures over 1,760°F (960°C). The resulting alumina powder goes to a refinery, where the pure metal is produced.

A typical Bayer plant will produce over 4,400 tons (4,000 tonnes) of alumina a day. Around 4 tons (tonnes) of bauxite will yield just over 2 tons (tonnes) of alumina.

Red-hot, molten aluminum is poured into molds to make ingots (bars) of the pure metal.

The Hall-Héroult process

The Hall-Héroult process is used to refine the alumina to aluminum. The process of using electricity to separate a metal from its rock ore is called electrolysis. This forms the basis of the second stage of aluminum production, which is called refining.

First, the alumina has to dissolve in a molten bath so that the aluminum and oxygen will break apart into electrically charged particles called ions. Aluminum has a positive charge. It can move through solutions toward the negatively charged

DOUBLE DISCOVERY

Charles Martin Hall's sister, Julia, was instrumental in developing the aluminum refining technique that bears the Hall name. In 1884, Charles read about the aluminum pyramid that was to form the tip of the Washington Monument and was then on display at Tiffany's. Excited by this new metal, brother and sister wondered if they could separate aluminum from bauxite using electricity. Their first efforts were frustrating, but on February 23, 1886, they finally succeeded, making marble-sized bits of aluminum. However, when Charles filed a patent in July, he found that Paul Héroult had patented an identical process in April of the same year.

Workers at a metal refinery in Kitimat, British Columbia, cover aluminum cylinders awaiting shipment overseas.

electrode of the bath, or cathode, which forms the lining to the bath. So, while a solid crust forms at the top of the bath, molten aluminum collects at the bottom, ready to be sucked out through a pipe.

Alumina is constantly piled onto the solid crust, where heat from the bath warms it up. Every so often the crust breaks, and the alumina falls into the molten liquid below. The baths are called "reduction pots" and are typically set out in long lines called potlines, each including 50 to 250 pots. The potlines are linked to one high-voltage electricity supply.

The aluminum drawn from the pots is 99.8 percent pure. All in all, about 4 tons (tonnes) of bauxite will make a ton of aluminum. Molten aluminum is drawn from the pots about once a day and cast

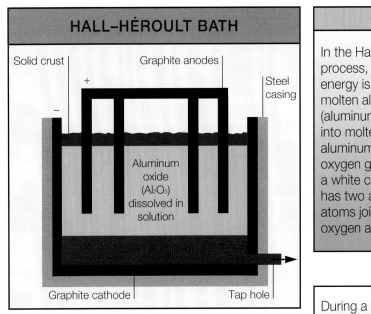

HALL–HÉROULT BATH

Solid crust

Graphite anodes

Steel casing

+

−

Aluminum oxide (Al₂O₃) dissolved in solution

Molten aluminum

Graphite cathode

Tap hole

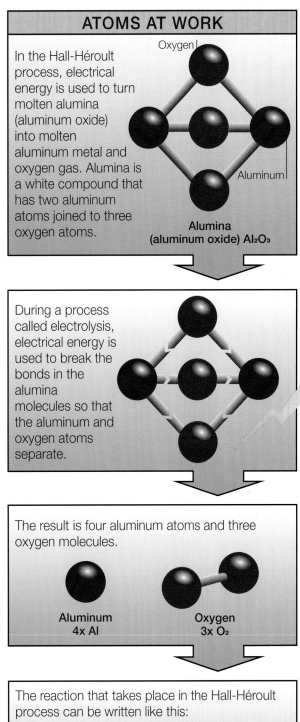

ATOMS AT WORK

In the Hall-Héroult process, electrical energy is used to turn molten alumina (aluminum oxide) into molten aluminum metal and oxygen gas. Alumina is a white compound that has two aluminum atoms joined to three oxygen atoms.

Oxygen

Aluminum

Alumina (aluminum oxide) Al₂O₃

During a process called electrolysis, electrical energy is used to break the bonds in the alumina molecules so that the aluminum and oxygen atoms separate.

The result is four aluminum atoms and three oxygen molecules.

Aluminum 4x Al

Oxygen 3x O₂

The reaction that takes place in the Hall-Héroult process can be written like this:

$$2Al_2O_3 \rightarrow 4Al + 3O_2$$

This equation tells us that two molecules of alumina will give four atoms of aluminum and three molecules of oxygen.

into huge ingots (bars) up to 30 ft (10 m) long. These are taken to other factories and made into various products.

Anodizing

Anodizing refers to the process by which aluminum is given a shiny protective coating to improve its looks. Aluminum is placed in a chemical bath containing dilute sulfuric acid (H_2SO_4). The aluminum acts as the positive electrode (anode). When an electric current flows through the bath, oxygen is given off at the anode. This combines with aluminum to form extra alumina on its surface.

Dyes are often mixed into the bath of sulfuric acid so that the coating can be made colorful and decorative. This is how a great deal of colored saucepans and other kitchenware is made.

Aluminum and its alloys

An airplane being built in the United States. Aluminum alloys are commonly used to make airplane parts, from the fuselage to the engine.

The properties of aluminum make it a very useful substance. It is soft and easy to shape, it is resistant to corrosion, it can be welded, and it forms alloys with other elements. As a result, the list of products that are made from aluminum is huge and includes everything from golf clubs to step ladders, paints to saucepans, and bottle caps to window frames.

Recycling aluminum

Although there is a huge quantity of aluminum still left in the ground, large areas of land have been devastated by bauxite mining. Moreover, making aluminum from bauxite uses a vast amount of energy. However, the demand for this useful metal is set to remain. As a result, recycling aluminum has become a major industry in many countries.

In the United States, almost a third of all aluminum is made from scrap—and almost half that is from beverage containers. Recycling saves about 95 percent of the energy used to make the same amount of aluminum from bauxite. By saving this energy, not only can resources such as coal and oil be

DID YOU KNOW?

STRANGE CRYSTALS

Quite recently, scientists discovered special crystals called quasi-crystals. These crystals appear to be a cross between glass and ordinary crystals. Quasi-crystals form in compounds noted for their high strength and light weight. Many scientists are convinced that they will soon be used in the aerospace industry. Aluminum seems especially prone to quasi-crystal formation, and nearly all the quasi-crystals made so far contain aluminum.

Crushed aluminum containers are prepared for recycling in Japan. The containers are processed into new sheets of aluminum.

conserved, but fewer pollutants, such as carbon dioxide and sulfur dioxide, are released by power stations. Today, recycling accounts for around 50 percent of the total use of aluminum.

Alloys

Pure aluminum is one of the lightest metals, so it will take less energy to move a piece of aluminum than, say, a piece of steel of the same size. This makes aluminum especially important in transport. If the steel parts of a vehicle are replaced with aluminum parts, less fuel is needed to move the vehicle, making it cheaper to run.

The only drawback is that pure aluminum is not a very strong metal. Combined with small quantities of various other elements in alloys, however, it becomes incredibly useful.

The most common aluminum alloys contain copper, magnesium, chromium, silicon, iron, nickel, and zinc. Each element adds its own unique properties to the final alloy. For example, magnesium makes the resulting alloy easier to weld. Silicon lowers its melting point and so makes it easier to cast. Copper makes the alloy stronger. Other alloy elements include cadmium, manganese, and titanium. In all cases, the proportion of added elements is less than 10 percent of the final alloy.

Wherever weight is of the essence, an alloy containing aluminum will often be used. Indeed, aluminum alloys are used to make airplane fuselages, automobile parts, racing bicycles, rockets, and wind turbines.

Aluminum and health

Compounds containing aluminum are sometimes found in small amounts in the human body. As far as scientists can tell, the human body has no use for aluminum compounds. Indeed, many physicians believe that the buildup of large quantities of aluminum compounds in the body may be harmful.

Stainless steel saucepans, pictured below, have largely replaced aluminum cooking utensils due to the unknown effects of aluminum in the body.

Aluminum can enter the body in a number of ways. For example, small quantities of aluminum can be swallowed. Antacid tablets, used as a remedy for indigestion, and toothpastes contain aluminum hydroxide ($Al[OH]_3$). Aluminum may be consumed if food is prepared using aluminum cooking utensils or cooking foil. Some foods contain additives such as potassium alum $(KAl[SO_4]_2)$, which is used to whiten flour. Aluminum may also enter through the skin. Aluminum chloride $(AlCl_3)$, for example, is used to make deodorants. Other compounds containing aluminum ions are often used as cosmetics.

In small quantities, there is no reason to believe that aluminum is harmful, and most aluminum is excreted from the body. However, some can build up in the brain, liver, lungs, and thyroid gland. People working in the aluminum and explosives industries, for example, may breathe minute drops of aluminum into their lungs, leading to lung diseases such as emphysema and fibrosis.

Aluminum on the brain

Many elderly people suffer from a form of dementia called Alzheimer's disease, which makes them increasingly forgetful, vague, and unable to cope with everyday life. There is some evidence that Alzheimer's disease is more common in areas where the water has a high aluminum content. Similarly, the brains of Alzheimer's sufferers seem to lack acetylcholine, a chemical that transmits nerve signals. Nerves that rely on this chemical play an important role in memory, and scientists have found high concentrations of aluminum in the same places. However, the evidence that aluminum is the cause is by no means overwhelming, and scientists have still not worked out if aluminum is the culprit.

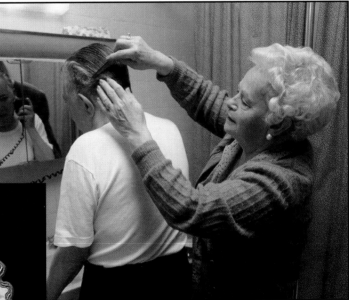

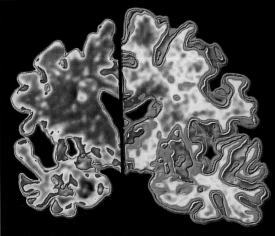

Above: An Alzheimer's patient needs the help of his wife to comb his hair.
Left: A computer-generated image of a vertical slice through the brain of an Alzheimer's sufferer (at left) is shown compared with a healthy brain (at right).

Periodic table

Everything in the universe is made from combinations of substances called elements. Elements are the building blocks of matter. They are made of tiny atoms, which are much too small to see.

The character of an atom depends on how many even tinier particles called protons there are in its center, or nucleus. An element's atomic number is the same as the number of protons.

Scientists have found around 110 different elements. About 90 elements occur naturally on Earth. The rest have been made in experiments.

All these elements are set out on a chart called the periodic table. This lists all the elements in order according to their atomic number.

The elements at the left of the table are metals. Those at the right are nonmetals. Between the metals and the nonmetals are the metalloids, which sometimes act like metals and sometimes like nonmetals.

● On the left of the table are the alkali metals. These elements have just one electron in their outer shells.

● On the right of the periodic table are the noble gases. These elements have full outer shells.

● Elements in the same group have the same number of electrons in their outer shells.

● Elements get more reactive as you go down a group.

● The number of electrons orbiting the nucleus increases down each group.

● The transition metals are in the middle of the table, between Groups II and III.

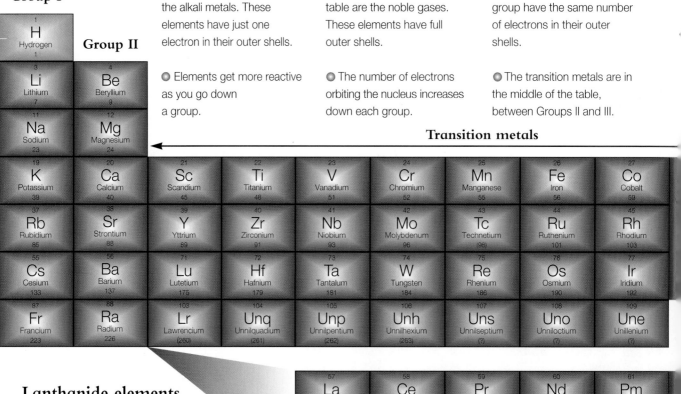

Group I

Group II

Transition metals

Lanthanide elements

Actinide elements

The horizontal rows are called periods. As you go across a period, the atomic number increases by one from each element to the next. The vertical columns are called groups. Elements get heavier as you go down a group. All the elements in a group have the same number of electrons in their outer shells. This means they react in similar ways.

The transition metals fall between Groups II and III. Their electron shells fill up in an unusual way. The lanthanide elements and the actinide elements are set apart from the main table to make it easier to read. All the lanthanide elements and the actinide elements are quite rare.

Aluminum in the table

Along with boron, gallium, indium, and thallium, aluminum forms Group III of the periodic table of elements. Each Group III element has three electrons in its outer shell, but they have very little else in common. They vary widely in the way they react with other chemicals, and, unlike the others, boron is not even a metal.

Chemical reactions

Chemical reactions are going on all the time—candles burn, nails rust, food is digested. Some reactions involve just two substances; others many more. But whenever a reaction takes place, at least one substance is changed.

In a chemical reaction, the atoms do not change. An iron atom remains an iron atom; an oxygen atom remains an oxygen atom. But they join together in different combinations to form new molecules.

Writing an equation

Chemical reactions can be described by writing down the atoms and molecules before and the atoms and molecules after. Since the atoms stay the same, the number of atoms before will be the same as the

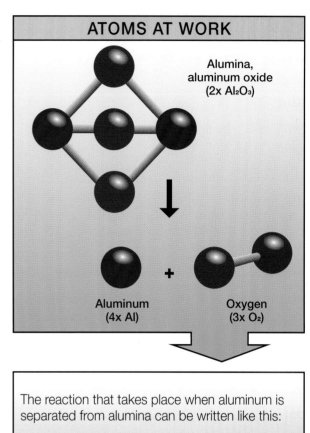

ATOMS AT WORK

Alumina, aluminum oxide (2x Al_2O_3)

Aluminum (4x Al)

Oxygen (3x O_2)

The reaction that takes place when aluminum is separated from alumina can be written like this:

$$2Al_2O_3 \rightarrow 4Al + 3O_2$$

Two molecules of alumina will give four atoms of aluminum and three molecules of oxygen.

number of atoms after. Chemists write the reaction as an equation. This shows what happens in the chemical reaction.

When the numbers of each atom on both sides of the equation are equal, the equation is balanced. If the numbers are not equal, something is wrong. So the chemist adjusts the number of atoms involved until the equation balances.

Alumina powder formed during the Bayer process. This compound is further refined to aluminum metal.

Glossary

alloy: A mixture of a metal with another element, often another metal.

amphoteric: Capable of reacting chemically either as an acid or a base.

anodizing: The process by which a metal is coated with a protective film to improve its looks.

atom: The smallest part of an element that has all the properties of that element.

atomic number: The number of protons in an atom.

bond: The attraction between two atoms that holds them together.

compound: A substance made of two or more elements that have combined together chemically.

corrosion: The eating away of a material by reaction with other chemicals, often oxygen and moisture in the air.

electrolysis: The use of electricity to change a substance chemically.

electron: A tiny particle with a negative charge. Electrons are found inside atoms, where they move around the nucleus in layers called electron shells.

igneous rock: A rock that develops from volcanic lava on Earth's surface or magma deep underground.

ion: A particle of an element similar to an atom but carrying an additional negative or positive electrical charge.

metal: An element on the left-hand side of the periodic table. Metals are good conductors of heat and electricity.

mordant: A chemical that combines with dyes and fixes them to other substances.

neutron: A tiny particle with no electrical charge. It is found in the nucleus of every atom.

nonmetal: An element on the right-hand side of the periodic table. Nonmetals are poor at conducting heat and electricity.

nucleus: The center of an atom. It contains protons and neutrons.

ore: A collection of minerals from which metals, in particular, are usually extracted.

periodic table: A chart of all the chemical elements laid out in order of their atomic number.

polarization: The state whereby a molecule possesses a positive electrical charge at one end and a more negative electrical charge at the other.

polymer: A long-chain molecule made up of repeating smaller units.

products: The substances formed in a chemical reaction.

proton: A tiny particle with a positive charge. Protons are found inside the nucleus of an atom.

reactants: The substances that react together in a chemical reaction.

refining: An industrial process that frees elements, such as metals, from impurities or unwanted material.

Index